RECYCLED ROBOTS

Dedicated to my grandfather, Hans Christian
Truelson, who taught me to respect simple tools
and building methods.

I would like to thank David Greenbaum, Fran Heyl,
Max Katz, and Herb Ohlmeyer for their various
helpful contributions to this book.

Copyright © 2012 by Robert A. Malone
Design copyright © by Workman Publishing

Library of Congress Cataloging-in-Publication Data is available.

ISBN: 978-0-7611-5466-2

Cover and box design by Raquel Jaramillo
Cover and box photo by Tae Won Yu
Interior design by Raquel Jaramillo
Interior photos by Melissa Lucier, Netta Rabin, and Tae Won Yu

Stock photography credits: p. 1, Hulton Archive/Getty Images; pp. 4 and 6, Photofest; pp. 7
and 8, Yoshikazu Tsuno/Getty Images; p. 9, Pascasl Goetgheluck/Photo Researchers, Inc.;
p. 11, Gianluca/Bloomberg via Getty Images; p. 12, Alexander Heimann/Getty Images; p. 13,
Purestock/Getty Images; p. 14 (left), UFA/The Kobal Collection/Art Resource; p. 14 (right),
Eduardo Parra/Getty Images; p. 15 (left), Walt Disney Pictures/Photofest; p. 15 (right):
COURTESY OF LUCASFILM LTD. *Star Wars: Episode IV – A New Hope*™ & ©1977 and
1997 Lucasfilm Ltd. All rights reserved. Used under authorization. Unauthorized duplication is
a violation of applicable law; p. 97, doll face (composite) Mel Yates/Getty Images.

Workman books are available at special discounts when purchased in bulk for premiums
and sales promotions as well as for fund-raising or educational use. Special editions or
book excerpts can also be created to specification. For details, contact the Special Sales
Director at the address below or send an e-mail to specialsales@workman.com.

Workman Publishing Company, Inc.
225 Varick Street
New York, NY 10014-4381
workman.com

Printed in China

First printing November 2012
10 9 8 7 6 5 4 3 2 1

RECYCLED ROBOTS

10 ROBOT PROJECTS

ROBERT MALONE

WORKMAN PUBLISHING
NEW YORK

CONTENTS

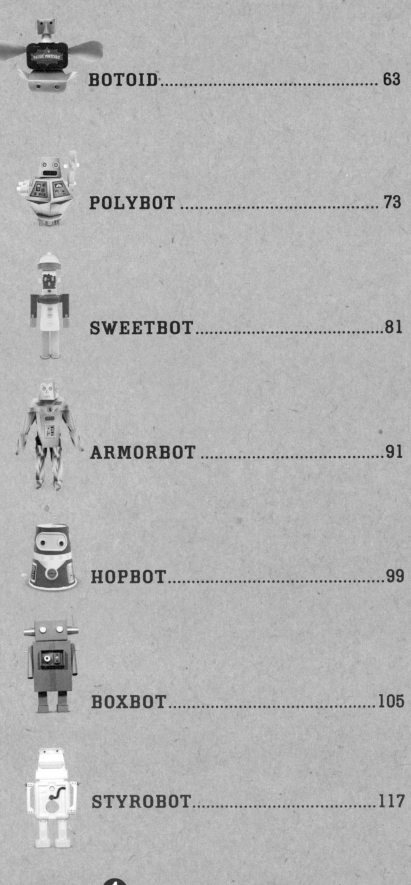

CHAPTER **4**
ROBOTS FROM ROBERT'S WORKSHOP.....129

THE THREE LAWS OF ROBOTICS*

A robot may not injure
a human being or allow a human
being to come to harm.

A robot must obey the
orders of human beings
except when it would
conflict with the First Law.

A robot must protect its own
existence as long as it does not conflict
with the First or Second Laws.

*Famous science fiction writer Isaac Asimov developed the Three
Laws of Robotics in his short story "Runaround." It outlines some
sensible rules for robots.

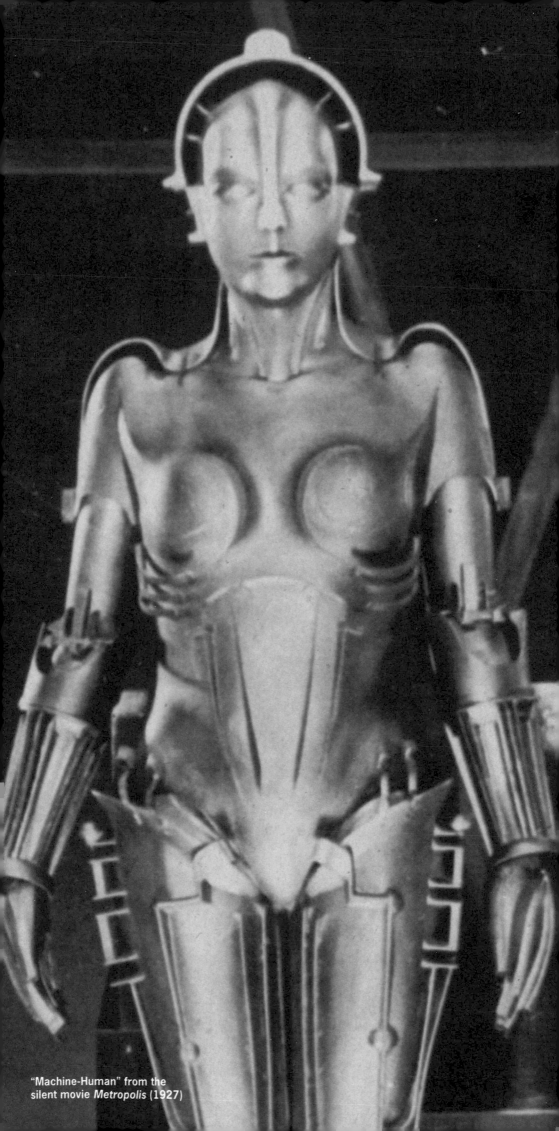

"Machine-Human" from the
silent movie *Metropolis* (1927)

INTROD

WHAT DO YOU think of when you hear the word "robot"? If you're like most people, you probably picture movie robots like R2-D2 and C-3PO from *Star Wars,* or Megatron from *Transformers.*

But what about a vacuum cleaner? Or a mechanical arm that can assemble a car? Or a flying bug as small as a flea? These days, robots are being used in more and more places to do important and interesting things. According to the International Federation of Robotics, there are an estimated 8.5 million robots moving and working everywhere in the world. That's twice the population of Kentucky! And the number is growing.

"In the simplest of terms, a robot is defined as a machine that acts and looks like a human…"

So, what exactly is a robot? In the simplest of terms, a robot is defined as a machine that acts and looks like a human or animal, or just a human or animal body part, like an arm or a leg (though there are some exceptions, like the Roomba® on pages 9–10.) A robot can be a toy, a game, a tool. It

02

RECYCLED ROBOTS

UCTION

can be all of these things or only some of them. Such a broad definition is a good thing, because it means that the possibilities are practically endless.

This book is all about exploring those possibilities. You don't need fancy equipment or a big laboratory or even a white lab coat to be an inventor, designer, and engineer of incredible robots. All you need are some basic art supplies and a lot of random things that you can find around your house, under the bed, behind a bookshelf, in the trash, and, of course, in recycling bins. Once you build some of the robots in the book, you'll come up with your own creative ways to hack your old toys and remote-control cars or repurpose your LEGO®s and action figures.

In other words, you'll start seeing possibilities in the stuff most people think of as "trash." That empty battery package your mom was going to toss out? It could make the perfect robot head. Those loose marker caps rattling around in your desk drawer? One of them could make a great robot nose. The trash you save from the landfill may only be a small fraction of the world's waste, but by reusing what you already have, you may be inspired to think about other ways you can consume less.

W. H. Richards's Universal Robot was the first British robot.

ROBOTS IN OUR WORLD

Inventor W. H. Richards and his R.U.R. shown having coffee

THE WORD "ROBOT" was first used in 1921 by Czech playwright Karel Čapek. In his play called *R.U.R.*, humans create humanlike beings (called "robots"), who are indistinguishable from humans and easily controlled. But soon the robots begin to develop thoughts and desires of their own. They organize a robot rebellion to overthrow their human overlords.

Since then, the idea that robots can think and act outside of human control has been a popular theme. And while robotics engineers are always pushing the boundaries of what robots can do, robots still can only act within the limits set up by the designer.

"Despite not being human, robots aren't quite machines, either."

But despite not being human, robots aren't quite machines, either. That's what makes them so fascinating. Gone are the days when robots were thought of as being clunky or stupid. Today, there are robots that can problem-solve, accomplish tasks on their own, process information, ask and answer questions, move and act with and without prompting, and even learn and interact socially.

One hundred years ago, writers and artists imagined a world in which robots walked among humans. That's not quite what happened, but they have become a big part of modern life.

Humanoid Robots

How far away are we from seeing real working, walking, talking humanoid robots (like the ones you see in the movies)? They're already here.

Some humanoid robots have the ability to control their actions internally, others by remote control. Some walking robots, like the ASIMO by Honda, are as large as humans. Honda's ASIMO robot has evolved significantly since it was introduced in 2000, going from a slow-walking robot with no "brain" to a faster walking bot with brains on board, and the ability to walk up a flight of stairs.

The Sony SDR-3X is another impressive humanoid robot. At only 20 inches tall and 10 pounds, this agile robot can walk, run, dance, and, when knocked down, get back up again. It can stand on one leg with its arms lifted to help balance itself, as if it were a gymnast. The SDR-3X has a camera inside its head, a microphone in each ear, and a speaker in its mouth. It can

The Sony SDR-3X walks, talks, and kicks a soccer ball.

say—and recognize—around twenty words. Its torso has sensors that help it to control its movements, and it can walk at a rate of about fifty feet per minute. There's also Toyota's Partner Robot, WALKING HUMANOID a humanoid bot that not only walks but plays a trumpet, violin, and drums.

Animal Robots

Robot designers don't just look to human forms for inspiration—the animal kingdom has just as many exciting possibilities. Sony's AIBO is a robot dog with amazing abilities and range of movement. The latest model, the AIBO Entertainment Robot, has expressive LED lights, a retractable headlight, stereo microphones for ears, a speaker for a mouth, a color camera, tail, and paws, and touch sensors. AIBO can be taught to respond and carry out complex actions like navigating through crowded environments.

Two Sony AIBOs play with a ball.

There is also the incredible BigDog which can walk over rough terrain with a heavy load, and RiSE V3, a catlike robot that crawls and can climb trees using mechanical claws.

The Active Scope Camera is a snakelike robot that can slither into tight spaces—such as through the debris after an earthquake.

Microrobots

At less than one millimeter in size (that's about the thickness of a dime), microrobots can explore areas that are too small or too dangerous for humans or larger robots. Some are as small as a microscopic piece of bacteria. Some can even fly! They are usually used in teams, similar to ants in an ant colony. They take their march-

This microrobot is about the size of an ant.

ing orders from a queen (in this case a control base run by a human or computer), and work together to achieve a goal.

Household Robots

The ROOMBA is a vacuuming robot equipped with a navigation system that allows it to move around obstacles, turn corners, and clean a floor from wall to wall. The disk-shaped ROOMBA combines imagination with top-notch engineering, programming, and design. Only a foot in diameter and a few inches tall, it is able to maneuver under sofas and beds while its owner is off doing something else.

Given the success of the Roomba, it's not surprising that there are other vacuum robots in various stages of development. There is also a steady increase in the number of robot lawn mowers, though

"In the future we may see robots that sweep, wash windows, blow snow, rake leaves, and hoe fields."

they are not as common. In the future we may see robots that sweep, wash widows, blow snow, rake leaves, and hoe fields. We may even use robots to replace our home security systems. Some of these will look like machines; others—particularly the home security robots—may look more like humans or pet animals.

This Roomba is the third model in the iRobot series.

Assembly Line Robots

Major appliances are, to a great extent, manufactured by robots. Robots assemble and weld cars, fit headlights and windows, even paint them. Many electronic products—MP3 players, cell phones, calculators, and digital cameras—are also made by robots.

Most industrial robots are fixed in one place and are programmed to do one action over and over at a speed and complexity that humans can't match.

The industrial Robotic Solutions AG robot wraps chocolate.

Robots that can do a job better, faster, and with more accuracy than a person are very valuable to manufacturers.

A good example of a modern industrial robot is the SCARA (Selective Compliant Assembly Robot Arm) robot. The SCARA, sometimes called the swivel-arm robot, has been designed to work in a way similar to a human arm. It has been applied worldwide to complex assembly work that requires a very high degree of precision and accuracy.

Investigative Robots

Originally developed to provide surveillance in dangerous areas of nuclear power plants, investigative robots are used by the police and security forces for surveillance. These sophisticated bots can enter places that are too risky for humans. They remove and dis-mantle bombs, and are often equipped with computers, vision systems, and navigational equipment that may be connected to satellites or other communication systems. They may also have manipulating arms and sensors that can test things like temperature, proximity, radiation, and even carry out chemical analysis.

OFRO, an investigative robot, scans a passenger at an airport.

Security robots like these can be adapted and simplified for use in homes and warehouses.

DRONES are unmanned flying robots that are popular in security and military fields. Powered by propellers or rotors, they resemble airplanes or small helicopters. They are computer programmed to be fully autonomous (self-acting) robots.

Exploration Robots

Some robots are built to go underwater, into space, and inside pyramids.

The first space robot was the LUNAR ROVER, which took some trips to the moon in the early 1970s. The VIKING 1 LANDER made it to Mars with a robotic arm to investigate the surface of the planet in 1976. Today, NASA robots like the MARS ROVERS are making very real contributions to our knowledge of outer space. The robot arm aboard the space shuttle helps maintain and repair earth satellites and the HUBBLE TELESCOPE.

Unmanned robots are used for deep-sea exploration. Oceanographer Robert Ballard's first underwater ships were manned, but eventually he developed JASON, a fully robotic underwater ship that can be sent to retrieve information from the ocean floor.

The PYRAMID ROVER was made to explore the Great Pyramid of Giza in Egypt. The ROVER is able to navigate through an ancient eight-inch-wide and six-hundred-foot-long interior passage, with its fiber-optic lens, high-resolution cameras, and smallest-ever ground-penetrating radar so it can go where no human—or bot—has been for at least 5,000 years.

The Mars Exploration Rovers are searching for signs of water on the red planet.

THE WAY WE USE robots in our world keeps changing as robots become more and more technologically advanced. At some point, robots may even begin thinking for themselves. This raises a lot of important questions: What uses do we have in store for them? How human will they get? How human will we want them to be? And what exactly will we have them do for us? People have a lot of different answers to these questions. What do you think?

Hollywood Robots

Robots first appeared in Hollywood in the 1920s and quickly became a science fiction staple. Good or evil, droid or cyborg, these red carpet–ready robots are always sure to entertain.

MARIA, THE "MACHINE-HUMAN,"
Metropolis
One of the first robots to grace the silver screen, Machine-Human was built by a mad scientist who wanted to resurrect his lost love, Maria. The robot can mimic the appearance of whomever her creator chooses.

THE TERMINATOR (aka T-800, T-850, T-101),
Terminator
Don't let the external layer of human flesh fool you. With a strong metal endoskeleton and the ability to shape-shift, this cyborg assassin sent back in time by the supercomputer Skynet is anything but human.

OPTIMUS PRIME, *Transformers*
When he's not a truck, Optimus Prime, the brave and compassionate leader of the Autobots, leads the fight against the Decepticons, evil robots bent on taking over the universe.

WALL-E, *WALL-E*
This friendly, trash-compacting robot is destined to a lonely life on an abandoned, waste-covered Earth until he falls in love with another robot, EVE, follows her to space, and subsequently restores life on Earth.

The "Machine-Human"

The T-850

HAL 9000, *2001: A Space Odyssey*
HAL is the ultimate bad robot. The onboard computer
responsible for maintaining all systems on the Discovery
One, HAL can interpret and reproduce emotional behavior
and reasoning, as well as play a mean game of chess with
the astronauts—that is, before HAL starts killing them.

R2-D2 & C-3PO, *Star Wars*
These two droids are always at a Skywalker's side, be it
Luke or Anakin. While C-3PO, a protocol droid designed
to serve humans, is fluent in over six million forms of
communication, R2-D2 prefers simple beeps to get his
point across.

ROSIE, *The Jetsons*
The Jetsons' robotic maid and housekeeper, Rosie goes
about her day on a set of caster wheels. Although she's an
outdated model, Mr. J and family would never let her go—
her discipline and wisdom is indispensable.

THE IRON GIANT, *The Iron Giant*
After crash-landing on Earth, the original Iron
Man befriends a young boy who teaches him to
speak English with the help of some *Superman*
comics. Afraid of his own strength, the Iron
Giant learns that a robot can be a hero, too.

WALL·E

WALL-E

R2-D2

C-3PO

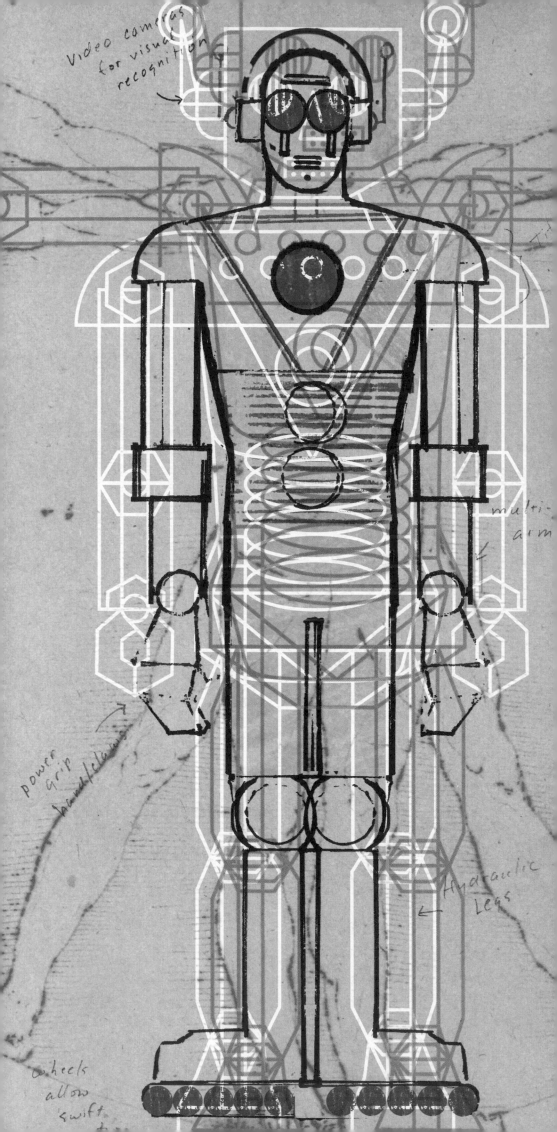

Video cameras for visual recognition

multi-arm

power grip hand/claw

Hydraulic Legs

wheels allow swift

CHAPTER 02

HOW TO DESIGN A ROBOT

ALMOST EVERY invention in the history of mankind, and certainly every work of art, probably began as a sketch: the most amazing machines ever made; the tallest buildings ever built; the longest bridges ever constructed. Rocketships. Sculptures. Toys. Everything started out as a person's vision, which was then transferred to a sketch. And from that first sketch, wonders emerged.

Designing Your Robot

A drawing, no matter how rough, is a way of imagining that opens the mind to possibilities, connecting the not-real-yet to the could-be-real in a visual way. A sketch helps you get your ideas down without worrying about the fussy details.

The design stage is essential to the practice of robotics. Scientists start with a simple sketch to get their ideas on paper and then decide which elements to move forward with and which to leave on paper.

"If you could design a real working robot, what would your robot look like?"

You should approach the creation of your robot the same way real scientists do: Start by sketching out your ideal robot. Do this before you even start building the robots in this book. Why? So that you can bring your own vision to all the robots you build. After all, just because robots aren't human doesn't mean they can't appear to have a little personality.

If you could design a real working robot, what would your robot look like? Do you like tough warrior robots or cute cuddly ones? Do you like robots that seem human, or do you prefer the ones that look like metal machines?

Leonardo da Vinci, the famous Renaissance artist, drew a diagram that showed that the length of a well-proportioned man's arms, when extended, are equal to his height.

If you want your robot to look somewhat human, sketch it out using the same "classic" proportions that artists often use as guidelines when drawing people. For instance, did you know that the average person is about seven times as tall as the length of his head?

The great thing about sketching your robot first is that it really helps you figure out not just how your robot will look, but also how it will work. Sketching and designing your robot helps you think about each element before you launch into building it, like what kind of body it will have, and how its arms will be attached, and how wide its shoulders should be. What kind of vision will it have? How will it move? What is its purpose? Will its purpose help shape what it looks like?

These are the kinds of questions you end up asking yourself as you start designing your robot.

START WITH A SKETCH!

RECYCLED ROBOTS

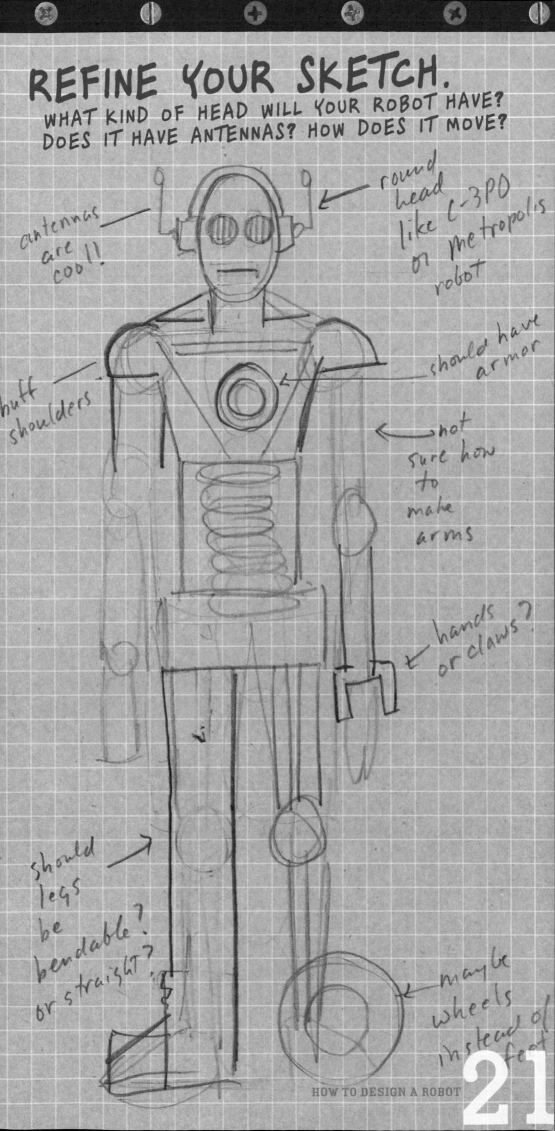

REFINE YOUR SKETCH.
WHAT KIND OF HEAD WILL YOUR ROBOT HAVE? DOES IT HAVE ANTENNAS? HOW DOES IT MOVE?

antennas are cool!!

round head like C-3PO or metropolis robot

buff shoulders

should have armor

not sure how to make arms

hands or claws?

should legs be bendable? or straight?

maybe wheels instead of feet

THINK ABOUT DETAILS.

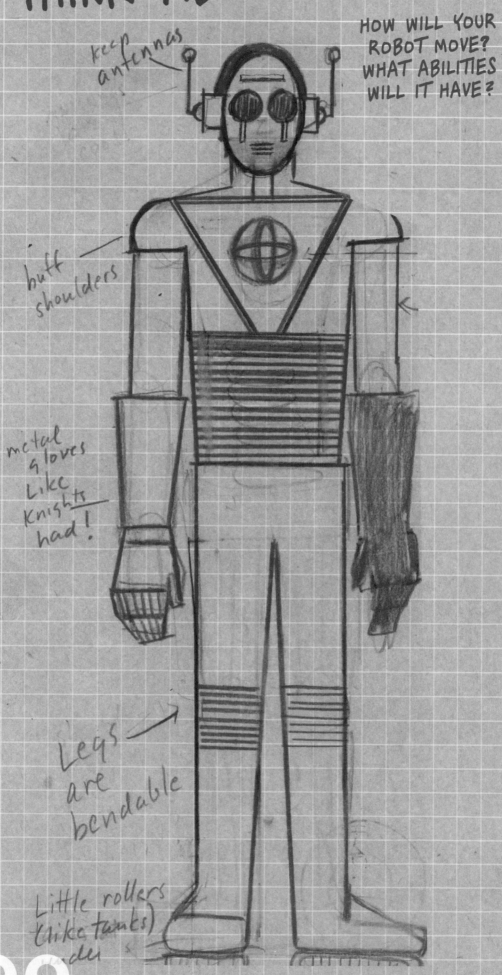

HOW WILL YOUR
ROBOT MOVE?
WHAT ABILITIES
WILL IT HAVE?

keep
antennas

buff
shoulders

metal
gloves
like
knights
had!

Legs →
are
bendable

Little rollers
(like tanks)
der

ADD THE FINISHING TOUCHES.

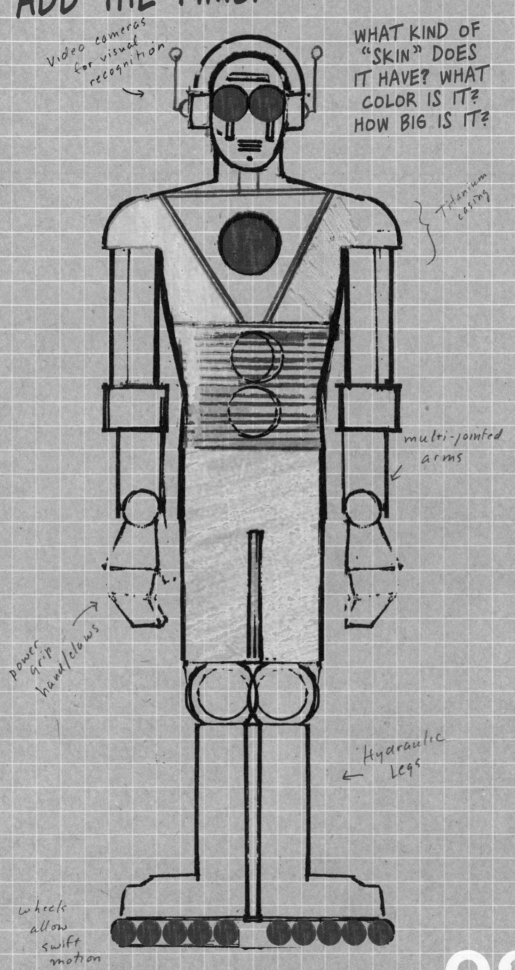

WHAT KIND OF "SKIN" DOES IT HAVE? WHAT COLOR IS IT? HOW BIG IS IT?

Video cameras for visual recognition

Titanium casing

multi-jointed arms

power grip hand/claws

Hydraulic Legs

wheels allow swift motion

NOW IT'S YOUR TURN!

START SKETCHING YOUR ROBOT ON THE FOLLOWING BLANK SKETCHBOOK PAGES. MAKE NOTES. THINK ABOUT MATERIALS. AND MOST IMPORTANT OF ALL, HAVE FUN!

26 RECYCLED ROBOTS

27

28 RECYCLED ROBOTS

29

CHAPTER 03

10 RE-CYCLED ROBOT PROJECTS

THE SKETCH IS the first step to making your robot. The next part is building it. This book tells you how to use recycled materials to build ten robots. Building these robots will show you ways to eventually build your own robot. So keep your robot sketches handy, and start building some of these recycled robots.

Building Your Robot

All the robot projects in this book have been designed to be as simple as possible. (They are robots, after all!) The instructions call for common household items and I have been as specific as possible with regard to the size and dimensions. They can all be made using the following tools:

- scissors
- white glue
- ruler
- pencil
- glue dots

- clear tape
- screwdriver
- hole punch
- pushpins

Finding Parts

You may not be able to find all the exact pieces that the robot projects call for. Don't let that stop you! (You're an inventor and inventors have to get creative.)

Start by looking in your room. You're sure to have old toys lying around. Can they be disassembled easily? Are there wheels you can use? What about old LEGO® pieces, TINKER-TOY® connectors, PLAY-DOH® containers? Do you have a remote-control car that might make the perfect way of mobilizing your robot? What about old school supplies, like tape dispensers or wire from the spiral note-book you used in science class last year?

Now check your kitchen. First try the recycling bin. That empty salt container would make the perfect torso for a robot, wouldn't it? Or that soup can. What about the cardboard tube in your roll of paper towels? Old plastic cups might come in handy, too. (Please thoroughly rinse them out first or your robot might end up being called Stinkbot!)

Expand your search to all the rooms in your house—even around your neighborhood. Is your neighbor throwing out the box his new computer came in? Well, get that pack-ing foam for your Styrobot (page 117). People discard all sorts of things, so keep an eye out for anything you might be able to repurpose.

Once you have your robot "parts," gather them together somewhere that's convenient. Try to find a workplace for your "robot workshop," a place where you can keep your tools and your materials. You can empty a few old shoe boxes for sorting your components.

Then, once you have your supplies, your parts, and your workplace, it's time to start building!

5 RULES FOR BUILDING ROBOTS

1. SHARP OR POINTY OBJECTS should never be handled without proper adult supervision.

2. WHEN USING SCREWS it's always best to start by making a starter hole—a smaller hole you can easily make with a pushpin. A pushpin is sharp, so you need adult supervision.

3. WHEN USING GLUE, only dispense a small amount. Hold both ends of what you are gluing tightly for at least three minutes. Never use glue that is not water-soluble or safe for kids.

4. IF CUTTING WIRE, use wire clippers, and always do this under adult supervision.

5. IF CUTTING CARDBOARD, do it slowly, always cut along a drawn line, and always do it under adult supervision.

RED

BOT

STOP SIGNS. FIRE ENGINES. TRAFFIC LIGHTS. No other color screams "Pay attention to me!" more than red. Mars is called the Red Planet because the iron dust that swirls around it gives its sky a reddish hue. The ancient Romans named the blood-colored planet Mars after their god of war.

Redbot isn't from Mars, but he could be. Almost all his parts are red, which makes digging around for the right junk something of a treasure hunt. Far from being a bloodthirsty god of war, he's a friendly guy. Who knew a packing tape dispenser came with such a happy smile?

RECYCLED MATERIALS
* 1 red hanging file folder
* 1 cardboard salt dispenser
* Assorted LEGO or TINKERTOY parts
* 2 red pencil grips
* 1 red packing tape dispenser

MATERIALS IN KIT
* Leg templates
* Mounting tape (cut to size)
* 2 googly eyes

TOOLS NEEDED
* Pencil
* Scissors
* Ruler
* White glue or tape
* Pushpin
* 2 screws
* Screwdriver

LEGS & BODY

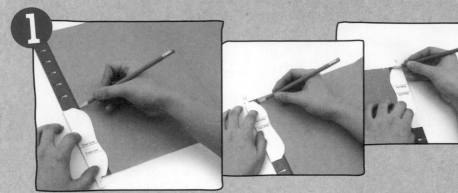

1 Using the Redbot **LEG** template, trace along the metal edge of the hanging folder as shown. Repeat two more times. Make sure that the template lines up with the metal hook each time.

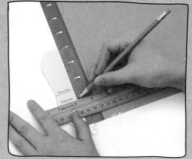

Be sure to transfer the **FOLD** and **GLUE** lines from the template onto the **LEG** shapes.

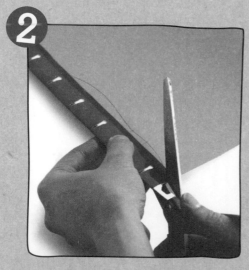

2 Cut out **LEGS**. There is a thin strip of metal at the edge that may be hard to cut through. You can ask a grown-up for help.

3 Fold along the **FOLD** line on each **LEG**.

4

Remove the wrapping from the salt dispenser. This will be Redbot's **BODY**. Measure the height of the salt dispenser and write it down.

5

Cut folder down the center fold. You now have two pieces.

6

On one piece of the folder, mark the length of the salt dispenser at each end as shown.

7

Draw a straight line connecting your dots.

8

Cut along the straight line.

9

Wrap the piece of red paper around the salt dispenser. Attach with tape or glue.

10

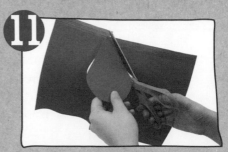

11

Cut out the circle.

Use the base of the salt dispenser to trace a circle on the remaining piece of hanging folder.

12

Apply glue and attach to top of salt dispenser.

13

Attach one LEG along the seam of the BODY. The top of the LEG should hit the middle of the BODY. Wait for glue to dry before attaching the other two legs. Each leg should be spaced evenly around the base.

14

Let all three legs dry thoroughly. A rubber band will keep legs in place as it dries.

THIS IS WHAT YOU SHOULD HAVE SO FAR.

ARMS

15

Using a **TINKERTOY** rod (or equivalent), insert one side of rod into pencil grip. This is Redbot's **ARM**.

16

Attach other **TINKERTOY** part (or equivalent) to the bottom of **ARM**. This is Redbot's **HAND**.

17

Cut a 1/4" slit into top of pencil grip.

18

Insert a screw through the slit so the end pokes out the other side, as shown.

19

With the pushpin, puncture a tiny hole on each side of **BODY**.

20

Using a screwdriver, attach **ARM** to side of **BODY** with a screw. Do not overtighten. Repeat steps 15–20 to make the other **ARM**.

HEAD & FACE

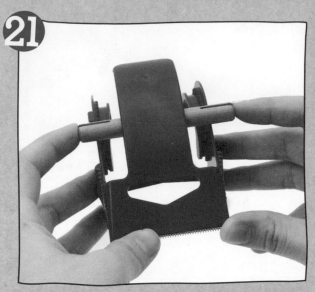

21

Use **TINKERTOY** rod (or equivalent) to create base for **EYES**. Wedge the rod behind top part of packing tape dispenser (Redbot's **HEAD**).

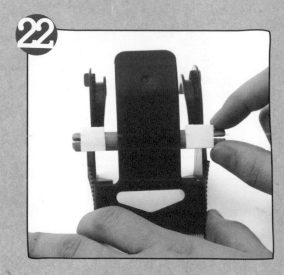

22

Apply mounting tape to each side of the rod.

23

Attach googly eyes as shown.

24 Use a **TINKERTOY** rod cover (or equivalent) to make Redbot's nose. Apply glue and attach to **HEAD** as shown (or position it wherever looks good to you).

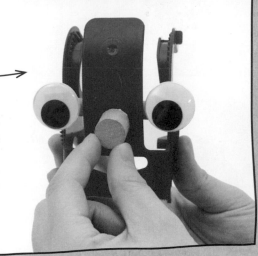

25 After eyes and nose have dried, add glue to base of **HEAD**.

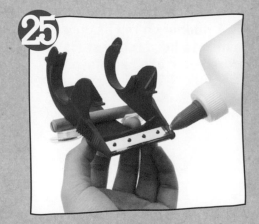

26 Attach **HEAD** to top of **BODY**. Add more glue as needed, and allow to dry for at least two hours. Glue round **TINKERTOY** part (or equivelant) to **REDBOT**'s chest.

MAKE IT GO!

A

Remove body of remote control car from the wheel base. You may need to pull hard.

B

Attach mounting tape to the top of the wheel base.

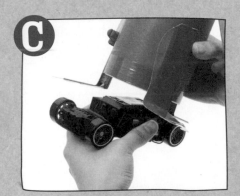

C

Place Redbot on top of the car. Make sure he is really stuck on before you make him move.

RECYCLED ROBOTS

EXTRAS

Attach other toy parts to decorate your Redbot's exoskeleton. For the Redbot on the left, I used a letter "O" refrigerator magnet as a chestplate and a piece of a curly keychain as an antenna.

You can use other materials to customize your Redbot. I made the Redbot on the right with a soup can and a mayonnaise jar lid, and used the metal parts of an old floppy disk for the eyes and the nose.

WEE

44 RECYCLED ROBOTS

BOT

THIS ITTY-BITTY BOT is the ultimate stealth spybot, accessing tiny, out-of-the-way crevices better than any human. Just make sure you keep a good eye on him. Once Weebot's all wound up, there's no telling where he might go.

Weebot proves that great things really do come in small packages—in this case, a small plastic container (PLAY-DOH cans fit best). You could also try a paper cup or even a toilet paper roll cut in half. We used LEGO pieces for his face, but you could also use buttons or beads.

RECYCLED MATERIALS
* I mini container
* I cap of a badminton shuttlecock
* I glue cap
* Assorted LEGO parts
* I drinking straw

MATERIALS IN KIT
* Mounting tape (cut to size)
* Windup motor

TOOLS NEEDED
* Aluminum foil
* Ruler
* Pencil
* Tape
* Scissors
* Glue dots

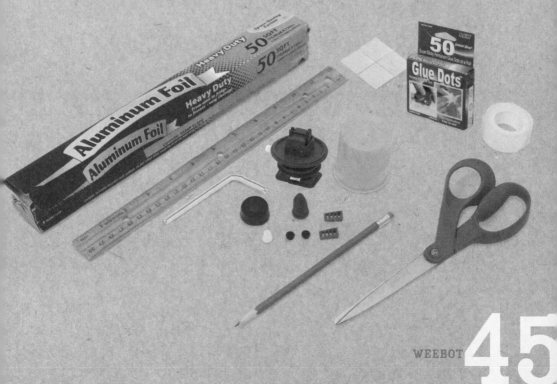

HEAD

1 Pull out a sheet of aluminum foil, at least 4" wide.

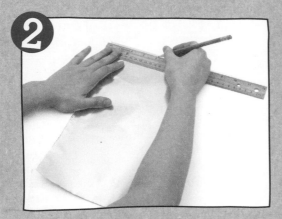

2 Measure and mark 4" on the short end of the sheet as shown.

3 Brace the ruler with your hand and tear off excess foil. Discard.

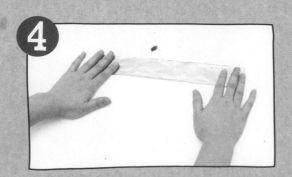

4 Fold the sheet of foil in half to reinforce it.

5

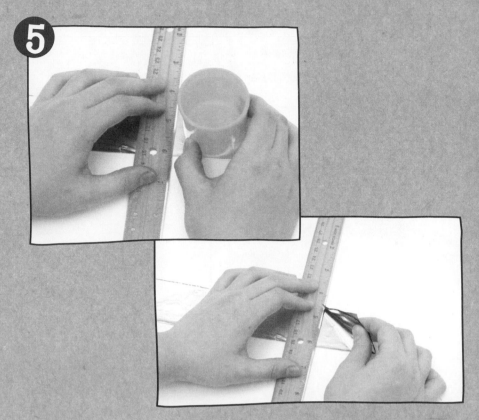

Place the container on one end of the foil strip. Place the ruler about $1/4"$ from the container. Set the container aside and tear off the small square of foil.

6

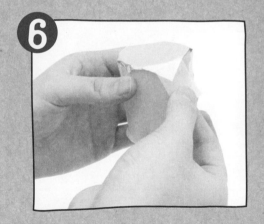

Place the square of foil on the bottom of the container and fold over the excess. Tape the four corners to the container. This will be the top of Weebot's **HEAD**.

7

Take the remaining strip of folded foil and tape one end to the side of the **HEAD**.

HEAD

8

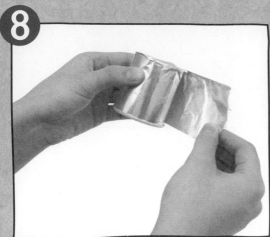

Wrap the foil around
the container and
tape down the end.

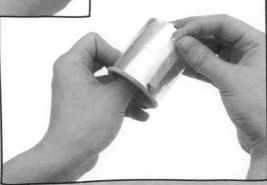

9

Apply mounting tape to the top
of the **HEAD** and attach a cap
from a badminton shuttlecock
(or equivalent). This will be
Weebot's hat.

FACE

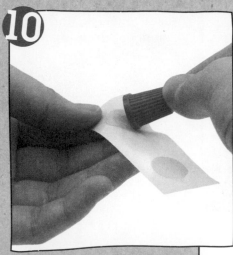

10

Apply glue dot to the
base of a glue cap and
attach it to Weebot's
FACE. This will be
Weebot's nose.

11

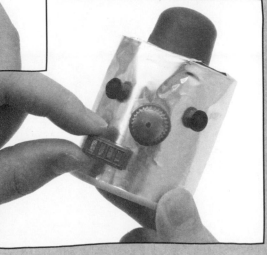

Attach small **LEGO**
parts to make eyes
and mouth for
Weebot. If you don't
have glue dots, you
can use mounting
tape cut to size.

LEGS & BODY

12

Measure, mark, and cut a 4" piece of drinking straw.

13

Attach the straw to the Weebot's back with strips of tape.

14

Cap the straw with a small **LEGO** piece or equivalent. This will be Weebot's antenna.

MAKE IT GO!

Place Weebot's **BODY** on to the blue windup walker. If your Weebot is too big for the walker, cut out and attach a circle of cardboard to the top of the walker to create a platform for Weebot. If your Weebot is too small, try lining the top of the walker with mounting tape and sticking him on.

Wind up the motor to make Weebot move!

CUP

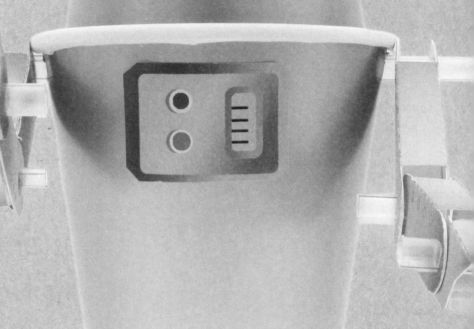

BOT

CUPBOT IS LIGHT, which makes him fast and perfect for racing. Match him against any rival robot and this deft droid is sure to win—or at least give his opponent a run for his money. Be careful, though: Cupbot can be a sore loser and those strong robot arms aren't anything to laugh at.

Make his titanium-like triceps with the template provided. If you can't collect any drinking straws, try pipe cleaners or twist ties that often come with garbage bags. If you don't have brass fasteners, try gluing on sequins or circles of tinfoil.

RECYCLED MATERIALS

* 3 paper cups
* 2 drinking straws
* 2 brass fasteners

MATERIALS IN KIT

* Cupbot arm templates
* Cupbot hand templates
* Chestplate sticker
* Mounting tape

TOOLS NEEDED

* Ruler
* Pencil
* Scissors
* Hole punch
* Pushpin
* White glue or tape

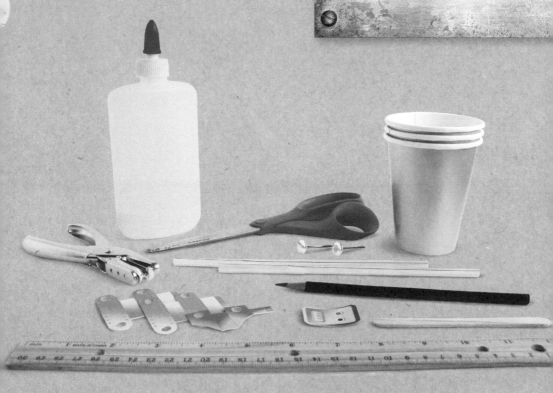

BASE

1 Measure I" from bottom of first cup. Mark the measurement in several places around the cup.

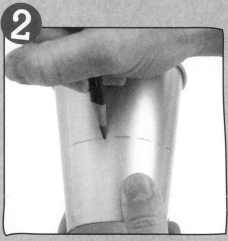

2 Connect the measurement marks so they form a circle around cup. This is where you will cut.

3 Use pencil to poke a hole through bottom of cup.

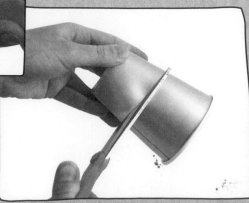

4 Insert scissors into hole. Cut up to and around the cut line. This will be Cupbot's BASE piece.

HEAD & BODY

5 Measure and mark 3" from bottom of the second cup. Mark the measurement in several places around cup. As in step 2, connect the marks to make a circle around cup.

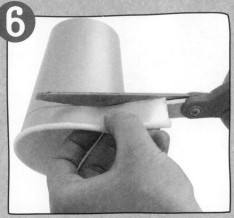

6 Cut up to and around your cut line. This will be Cupbot's **HEAD**.

7 Using a hole punch, make a hole under the third cup's rim.

8 Widen the hole slightly by punching another hole slightly to the side. The circle must be large enough for a straw to fit through. This will be Cupbot's **BODY**.

BASE

HEAD

BODY

THIS IS WHAT YOU SHOULD HAVE SO FAR.

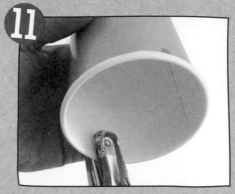

Measure, mark, and cut a 5" piece of straw.

Insert straw through the HEAD cup's hole. Trace where the straw meets the inside of the cup.

Double punch holes at the mark, as in step 8.

Insert the HEAD cup into the BODY. Line up the cup's seams (if it has them).

Trace the BODY hole onto the HEAD. Do this on both sides.

Double punch holes through both marks on the HEAD.

FACE & SHOULDERS

Turn the **HEAD** so the shoulder holes are at the sides. Mark Xs where you'd like the eyes to go.

Use a pushpin to punch starter holes in the center of the Xs (you may want to make a few). Insert brass fasteners into eye holes.

Secure brass fasteners to the inside of **HEAD**.

Place **HEAD** into the **BODY** and insert the 5" straw piece through both holes. This will attach **BODY** to **HEAD** and give Cupbot **SHOULDERS**. You may want to stick a pencil through the holes to make it easier.

ARMS & HANDS

19

Punch out and fold **ARM** and **HAND** templates.

20

Apply glue to gray areas. Fold close and wait for glue to dry.

21

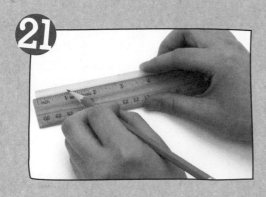

Measure, mark, and cut four I" pieces of straw.

22

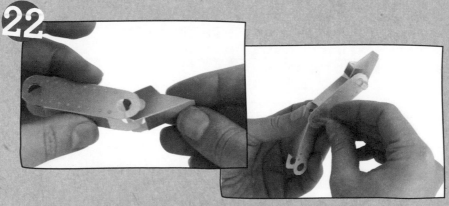

Use the pieces of straw as joints to attach the **HANDS** to the **LOWER ARMS** and the **LOWER ARMS** to the **UPPER ARMS**.

THIS IS WHAT YOU SHOULD HAVE SO FAR.

UPPER ARM

LOWER ARM

HAND

23 Insert the **ARMS** onto both **SHOULDERS**.

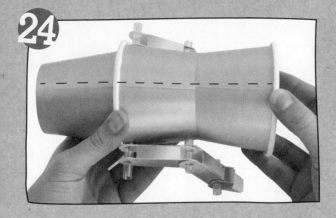

24 Insert **HEAD** and **BODY** onto the **BASE**. Line up back seams.

25 Attach the chestplate sticker to Cupbot's chest (or wherever you think looks good).

MAKE IT GO!

A

To make Cupbot move, find a lid that will fit into the body (we used a cap to a mayonnaise jar) and a pull-back car that fits under the lid. The pull-back car should have as flat a top as you can find.

B

Add mounting tape strips to the inside of the lid and to the top of the car. You can also use mounting tape.

Insert lid into Cupbot's BASE.

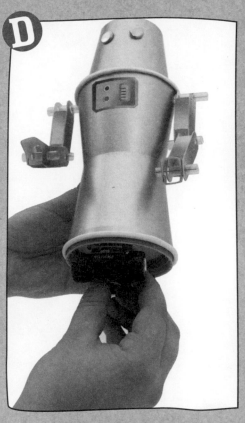

Attach BASE to the car and Cupbot is ready to roll!

ALL NATURAL INGREDIENTS

MAISIE MINTOIDS

SPEARMINT

NET WT 2 OZ

OID

BOTOID IS A MODERN TAKE on the traditional tin robots popular with kids in the 1950s and 1960s. Use the gold metallic templates provided to create her giant, oarlike arms and watch out! This robot is no pushover. In fact, she's more likely to push other things over.

Any fun-looking metal or plastic candy box will work. For her antennae, try paper clips, toothpicks—anything that's straight and skinny—and light!

RECYCLED MATERIALS

* I candy tin or box
* I drinking straw
* 2 brass fasteners

MATERIALS IN KIT

* Botoid templates
* Mounting tape (cut to size)
* Three 1½" dowels
* One 10" dowel
* I wooden bead

TOOLS NEEDED

* White glue
* Ruler
* Scissors
* Pencil

1

Punch out Botoid's **HEAD** template. Punch out the eye, and neck holes, and fold on all dotted lines.

2

Apply glue to gray areas. Fold and attach tab A to A, then tab B to B. Finally, tuck in tab C to C.

3

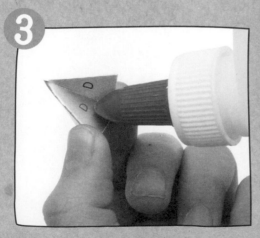

Punch out **NOSE** template. Fold on dotted lines and apply glue to gray areas. Attach tab D to D.

4

Attach **NOSE** to **HEAD**, matching E to E. Hold for a minute while glue dries.

5 Cut two pieces of mounting tape, each about 1/4" wide and 3/4" long.

6 Attach tape to both sides of Botoid's HEAD.

7 Attach a 1 1/2" dowel to each side.

8 Punch out NECK template.

9 Fold open the four small flaps and curve into cone shape. Apply glue to gray area and close, matching A to A. Hold for a few minutes to let glue dry. You can also use a paper clip.

10 Insert NECK into HEAD until it snaps into place.

BODY & ARMS

11

Apply mounting tape to the top center of mint tin or equivalent. This is the **BODY**.

12

Attach the wood bead to the mounting tape. Then insert a 1½" dowel through the hole.

THIS IS WHAT YOU SHOULD HAVE SO FAR.

13

Place mounting tape across the back of the **BODY**.

14

Measure, mark, and cut a 3¾" piece of straw.

15

Center and attach straw to mounting tape.

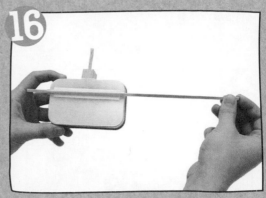

16

Insert the 10" dowel through the straw.

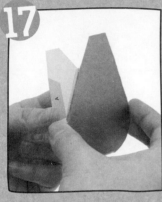

17

Punch out **ARM** templates and fold on dotted lines.

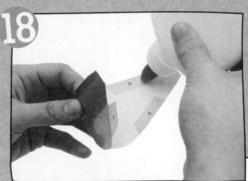

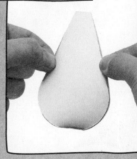

18

Apply glue to gray areas. Fold tab A to meet A and tab B to meet B. Hold for a minute while glue dries.

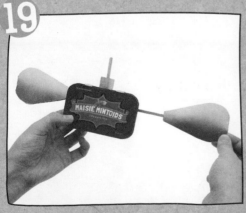

19

Slip **ARM** onto the dowel. Repeat on other side.

20

Insert the **HEAD** and **NECK** onto the dowel.

21

Punch out BASE template and
fold on the dotted lines. Punch
out starter holes on the front of
the BASE.

22

Insert brass fasteners into
starter holes and secure
brass fasteners as shown.

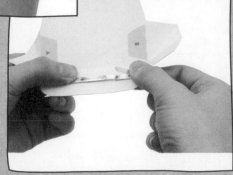

23

Fold on lines, to create the "wings" of the BASE. Apply glue to gray areas. Fold tabs A to A, B to B, C to C, and D to D.

24

Attach mounting tape to bottom of BODY.

25

Attach BODY to middle of BASE. You may need to fold up the "wings" of the BASE.

MAKE IT GO!

A Remove body of remote control car from the wheel base. You may need to pull hard.

B Attach mounting tape to the top of the wheel base.

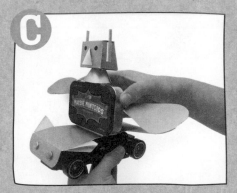

C Stick robot to the mounting tape so that the front lip covers the front of the wheel base.

EXTRAS

Here I tried a variation using a different-shaped tin. You can also use a plastic container wrapped in aluminum foil to give it a metallic look.

POL

YBOT

POLYBOT IS A ROBOT OF MANY SIDES. He may be a machine, but his unique shape comes from the natural world. Polybot is shaped like a hexagon, just like snowflakes, honeycomb, and the back of a turtle's shell. No wonder Polybot is one of the most graceful robots around.

Check out his feet! Polybot uses ingenious brush motors to get around like a pro.

RECYCLED MATERIALS

* I drinking straw

MATERIALS IN KIT

* Polybot template
* Brush motor
* Mounting tape (cut to size)

TOOLS NEEDED

* White glue
* Pencil
* Ruler
* Scissors

HEAD & FACE

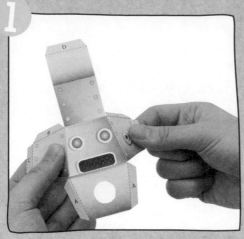

1

Punch out Polybot's HEAD and fold on all dotted lines.

2

Fold in at the tabs and apply glue to gray areas.

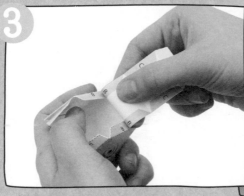

3

Fold tabs A to meet A. Fold tabs B to B and tabs C to C and tab D to D. Hold for a couple of minutes while glue dries.

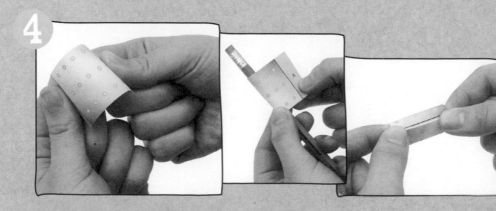

4

Punch out the NECK template and roll into a tube. A pencil can help with this.

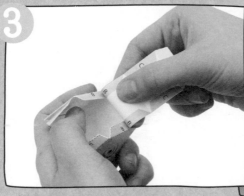

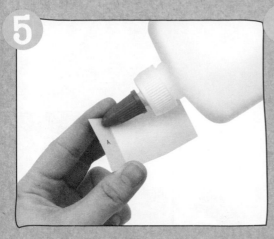

5

6

Apply glue to gray area and attach **A** to **A**. Hold for a minute while glue dries.

Pop open the Polybot's **BODY**.

7

Insert **NECK** into the hole at the top of the **BODY**.

8

Insert **NECK** into **HEAD**.

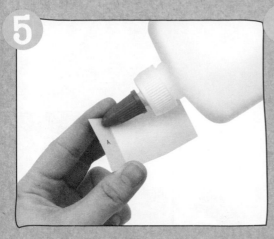

POLYBOT **75**

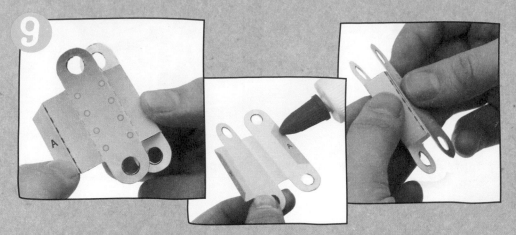

9

Punch out **ARM** templates and fold on all dotted lines. Apply glue to gray area of first **ARM** and fold tab **A** to **A**. Repeat with second **ARM**.

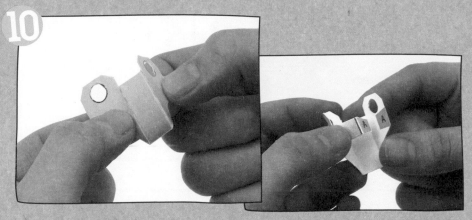

10

Punch out **HAND** templates and fold on all dotted lines. Apply glue to gray area and fold tab **A** to tab **A**. Hold for a minute while glue dries.

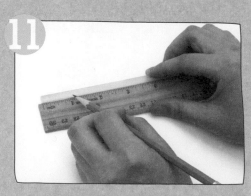

11

Measure, mark, and cut two I" pieces of straw.

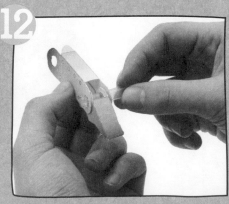

12

Line up **HAND** holes with **ARM** holes and insert straw to attach.

BODY

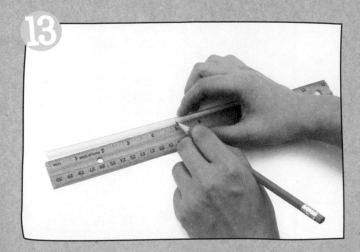

13 Measure, mark, and cut one 5" piece of straw.

14 Insert 5" straw through holes on either side of Polybot's **BODY**.

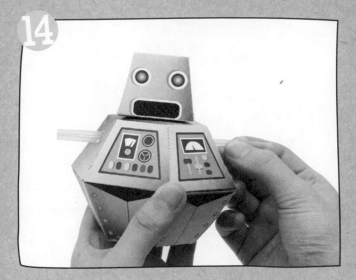

15 Attach **ARMS** onto each side of the straw.

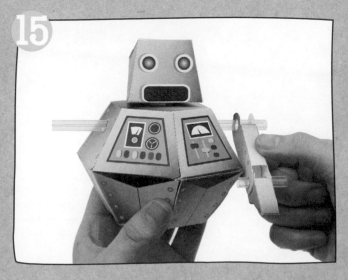

MAKE IT GO!

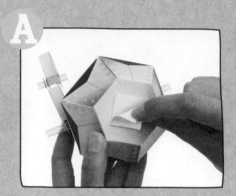

A Apply mounting tape to the bottom of Polybot's **BODY**.

B Center the **BODY** over the base of the brush motor.

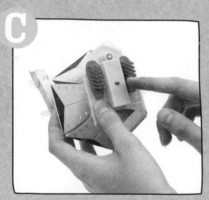

C Attach the two pieces together by pressing firmly. It's important to get the balance right. If Polybot topples over, adjust the motor's placement until you find the sweet spot.*

EXTRAS

Design your own Polybot using the blank polyhedron in the kit. You can make it go with the motorized base that comes in the kit—or use any Bristlebots or **HEXBUG**® Nanos you have lying around your room. That way you can have a battle of the Polybots! Who will win?

*If your brush motor battery runs out, replace it with two LR44 button cell batteries. Ask a parent for help removing the screws.

SWE

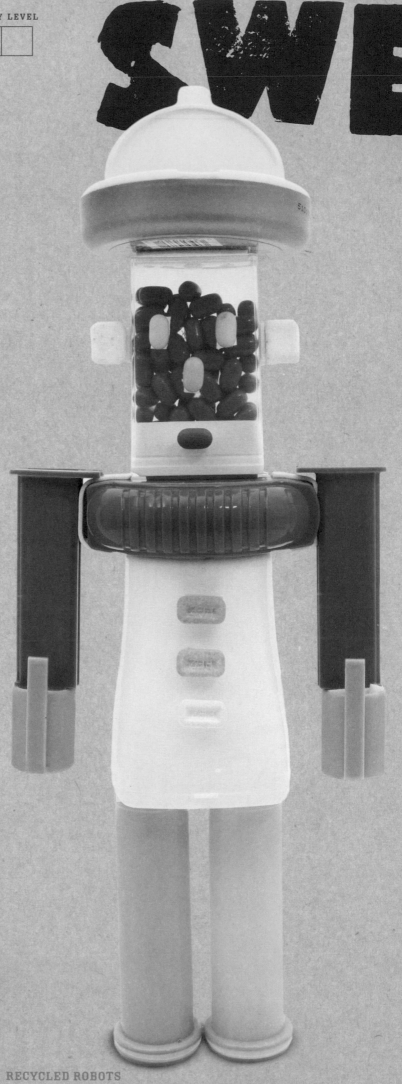

ETBOT

SWEETBOT IS A TOTAL sweetheart inside and out, but this retro-looking robot proves that sweetness packs a strong punch. His brawny plastic body is no match for many punier bots, and he can go head-to-head with almost any recycled robot out there. But he'd much rather lounge around the house and munch on some sugary treats.

You can make Sweetbot out of a variety of candy packaging. Search the house for all the empty candy containers you can find. Sketch out what you have and improvise. Just make sure you remember proportions—make Sweetbot too top-heavy and he'll topple over. The sky (or your sweet tooth) is the limit!

RECYCLED MATERIALS

* Assorted candy containers
  You'll need the following shapes:
  LEGS: 2 tall, skinny containers (Make sure they can stand up on their own.)
  BODY: I medium mint container with a wide base
  HEAD: I small square box
  NECK: I round dispenser
  HAT: I round dispenser
  ARMS: 2 long, skinny containers
  HANDS: 2 plastic caps (These can be found on some types of candy containers, but marker caps also work.)
* Assorted pieces of small hard candy

MATERIALS IN KIT

* Mounting tape (cut to size)

TOOLS NEEDED

* Scissors

LEGS & BODY

1

Place **LEGS** lid-side down, with the lid openings facing front.

2

Apply mounting tape to the top of both **LEGS**.

3

Attach **BODY**, lid-side down to both **LEGS**.

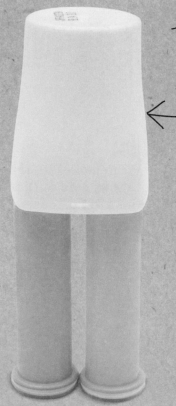

THIS IS WHAT YOU SHOULD HAVE SO FAR.

4

Apply mounting tape to top of **BODY**.

5

Attach **NECK** to top of **BODY**. Make sure the **NECK** container is centered on the **BODY**.

6

Apply a strip of mounting tape to each side of **NECK**. The tape should overlap the top by $1/4$".

ARMS & HANDS

7

Wrap mounting tape (sticky side out) around the ARM pieces.

8

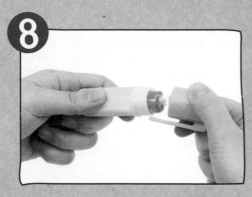

Remove the HAND caps from their base.

9

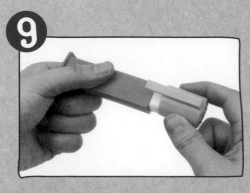

Attach HANDS to ARMS with the cap clip facing front, as shown.

10

Attach ARMS to NECK.

HEAD

11

Apply mounting
tape to box lid.

12

Attach **HEAD** to **NECK**,
lid-side down.

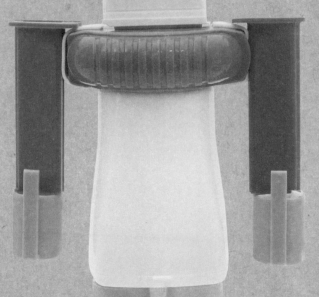

THIS IS WHAT YOU
SHOULD HAVE SO FAR.

13

Apply mounting tape to top of **HEAD**.

14

Attach **HAT** to **HEAD** with lid of **HAT** open and sticking up.

THIS IS WHAT YOU SHOULD HAVE SO FAR.

BODY & FACE

15

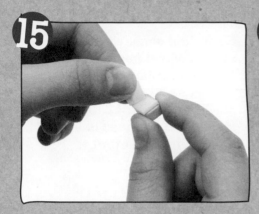

Apply mounting tape to three small pieces of hard candy.

16

Attach candies to **BODY** as shown.

17

Apply mounting tape to four more pieces of hard candy. These will be the **EYES**, **NOSE**, and **MOUTH**. Attach to Sweetbot's **HEAD**.

18

Apply mounting tape to each side of the **HEAD** as shown.

19

Attach two mints. These are Sweetbot's **EARS**.

MAKE IT GO!

A

First, find some wheels. I had a wheel base from a broken pull-back car. You could use a remote control car like on page 42. Just make sure the base is big enough for Sweetbot to stand on it.

B

Apply mounting tape to the bottom of Sweetbot's legs.

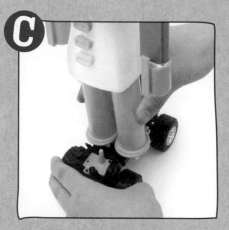

C

Attach him to the pull-back car and watch him go!

EXTRAS

Sweetbot is a good example of how the same materials can be reassembled to make a robot with a whole different look. I also took apart a mini mint tin to give him a hat and a smile.

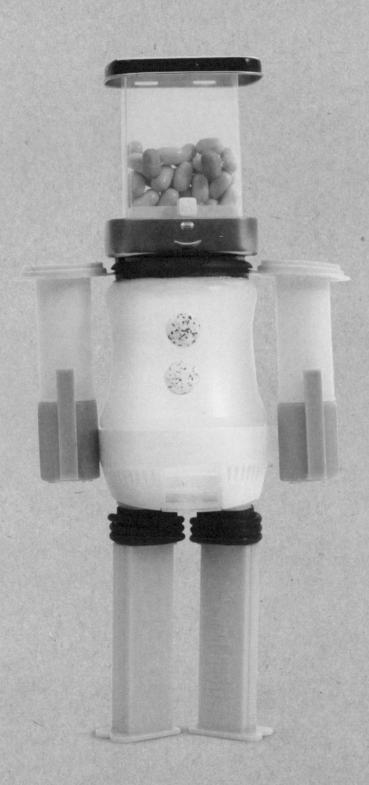

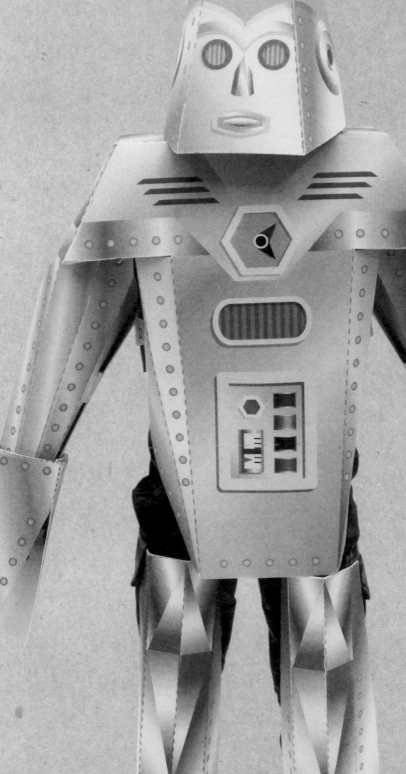

ORBOT

MEET ONE TOUGH ROBOT. What Armorbot lacks in mobility, he more than makes up for in strength. Nothing gets past his solid, full-body shield. Armorbot's exoskeleton, or outer shell, is designed to be superstrong, yet lightweight enough for him to get around.

Use the Armorbot templates included in the kit to create the ultimate body shield for an old action figure or a small doll. Once Armorbot is all suited up, he knows no bounds.

RECYCLED MATERIALS
* 1 action figure or
  1 small doll

TOOLS NEEDED
* White glue
* Pencil

MATERIALS IN KIT
* Armorbot templates

HEAD

1

Punch out Armorbot's HEAD template and fold on all dotted lines.

2

Apply glue to gray areas marked A and B.

Fold tab A to meet A. Hold for a minute while glue dries. Tuck in the B tabs to meet B. Hold for a few minutes until glue dries.

CHEST

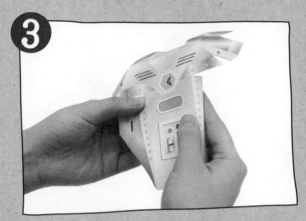

3 Punch out CHEST template. Punch out neck hole and slots marked C and D. Fold on dotted lines.

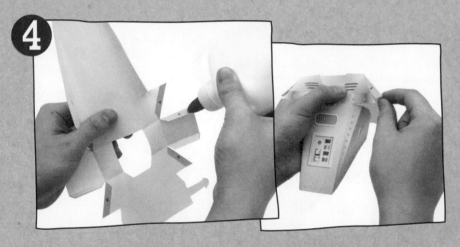

4 Apply glue to all gray areas marked A and B. Attach tabs A to A and tabs B to B. Hold down for a few minutes until the glue dries.

5 Insert Armorbot's HEAD through the neck hole. Slip tabs C and D through slots C and D as far as they will go.

ARMS

6

Punch out **ARM** templates and fold on the dotted lines.

7

Wrap templates around action figure's **ARM** and insert the A tabs into the A slots as far as they will go.

8

Punch out **PINCER** templates and fold on all dotted lines.

9

Apply glue to gray areas. Fo' close, so tab A meets A.

Push in the four tabs as sho Wait until the arms have fu dried before moving on to t next step.

10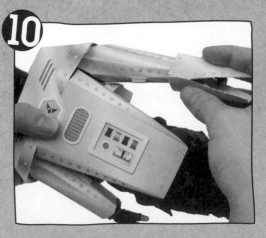

Insert your **PINCERS** into the **ARMS** by fitting your action figure's hands through the four tabs.

LEGS & FEET

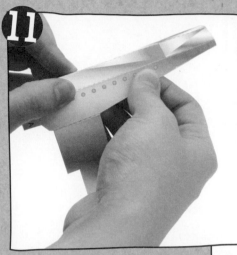

11

Punch out **LEG** templates and fold on all dotted lines.

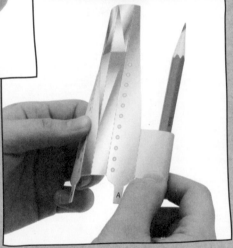

Use a pencil to curve the gray B tab. This will wrap around the figure's leg.

12

Punch out **FEET** templates and fold on all dotted lines.

13

Apply glue to gray areas marked C, then fold closed so C meets C. Hold until glue dries.

14

Attach **FOOT** to **LEG** by inserting the tabs into the **A** slots. Repeat with remaining **FOOT** and **LEG**.

15

Attach **LEG/FOOT** piece to figure by fitting around leg and inserting the **B** tab into the slot as far as it will go. Repeat on other side.

16

Complete your Armorbot by putting on his **HEAD**.

EXTRAS

Experiment with fitting Armorbot onto different action figures or dolls.

HOP

BOT

S OME BOTS CAN climb stairs, other bots can march or run or dance—this little guy hops. He may not be fast, he may not be graceful, but give him a destination and a little bit of time, and he'll get there eventually.

This project is pretty simple. If you don't have a paper cup, a plastic one will work, too. When Hopbot isn't on the move, he looks pretty cute just sitting on the shelf with that curious little look on his face.

RECYCLED MATERIALS
* I paper cup

MATERIALS IN KIT
* Decals
* Googly eyes
* Motor
* Wire
* Mounting tape (cut to size)
* Bead (you can paint it a fun color)

TOOLS NEEDED
* Pushpin
* Hole punch
* Tape
* Scissors
* Ruler
* Pencil

HEAD & FACE

1

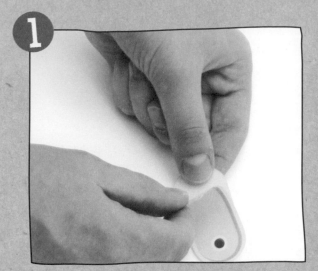

Peel away the adhesive backing to the Hopbot decals as you need them.

2

Apply the EYES decal about $^1/_4$" inch from the top of the cup. Make sure that it is straight!

3

Apply the CHEST plate, centering the lower circle between the eyes as shown.

4

Apply the EARS, one to each side of Hopbot's HEAD.

5

Apply the blue control panel decal on the left side of the robot as shown.

6

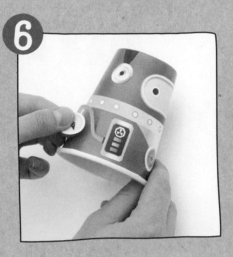

Apply the red control panel decal on the right side of the robot.

7

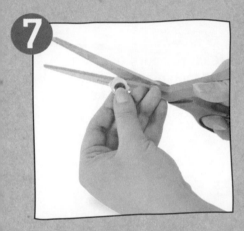

Apply mounting tape to both googly eyes and cut away the excess tape.

8

Apply googly eyes over each EYE on the decal.

THIS IS WHAT YOU SHOULD HAVE SO FAR.

ANTENNA

9

With a pushpin, make a hole on the center of Hopbot's head.

10

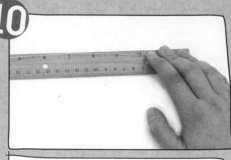

Measure, mark, and cut a 10-inch piece of wire. Wrap wire around pencil to create a spiral.

11

Thread about 1" of wire through the bead. Bend the wire and twist the bead to secure it as shown.

Insert wire into the hole on Hopbot's head. Tape down the excess wire (about 1") to the inside of the cup with a piece of tape.

12

MAKE IT GO!

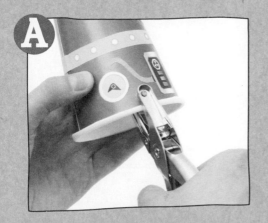

A Using a hole punch, make a hole on the left side directly above the rim of the cup and in line beneath Hopbot's left ear.

B Apply mounting tape to the red windup walker. Make sure the tape is to the left of the winder, as shown.

C Insert the handle of the windup walker through the hole and attach to the inside of the cup.

Fully wind the motor to make Hopbot hop!

BOX

BOT

BOXBOT IS SO INCREDIBLE, it's hard to imagine that he's made up of old cardboard boxes. He even has a rotating head and movable arms!

Don't worry if your boxes don't match the ones I used. Just be sure you think about scale—the BODY box should be bigger than the HEAD box so your Boxbot doesn't topple over. If your box has writing on it, you can paint him silver or bright orange or pink. If you don't have jewels for his controls, try using bottle caps, buttons, beads, or even LEGO® pieces. Boxbot is endlessly adaptable, which makes him a really fun robot to build.

RECYCLED MATERIALS
* 10 assorted boxes and tubes:
  * **HEAD:** 1 medium box
  * **BODY:** 1 big box
  * **ARMS:** 2 paper towel tubes
  * **LEGS:** 2 mini cereal boxes
  * **FEET:** 2 small boxes of equal size
  * **CONTROL PANEL:** 1 scrap of cardboard and 1 small or medium box without a top
* 1 set of chopsticks
* Round, 2" cap
* 6 paper cups
* Wooden push-along toy or object with equivalent rod
* Plastic jewels or equivalent

MATERIALS IN KIT
* Mounting tape (cut to size)

TOOLS NEEDED
* Packing tape
* Pencil
* Ruler
* Pushpin
* Scissors
* White glue

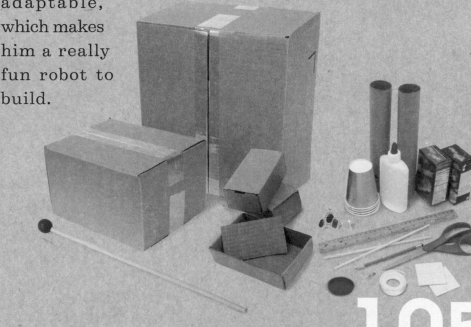

HEAD

1

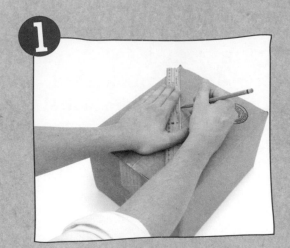

Seal both sides of a medium box (the **HEAD**) with packing tape. **On the bottom side of the box, find the center by drawing an "X" from one corner to the other as shown.**

2

At the center of the "X," trace a circle using the 2" cap as your guide.

3

Using a pushpin, make pinholes around the circle. They should be very close together.

4

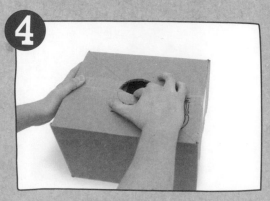

Push in the circle with your finger to create a round neck hole.

& EYES

5 Measure and mark I" from bottom of a cup. Repeat this mark several times around the cup.

6 Connect your marks so they make an even circle around the cup. You will cut along this line.

7 Cut up the side of the cup and around the cut line. Repeat steps 5–7 with a second cup. These will be Boxbot's EYES.

8 Apply glue to the cut edge of each EYE.

9 Place the EYES on the robot HEAD and let dry.

EARS

10

With a new cup, measure and mark 2" from the bottom. This will be one of Boxbot's EARS.

11

With a pushpin, make a starter hole at the mark.

12

Insert chopstick through the hole. Make a mark where the chopstick meets the inside of the cup, as shown.

13

Make a starter hole with pushpin. Then insert chopstick through the two holes.

14

Apply glue around the rim of the cup.

15

Place cup to the side of the head and let dry completely. Repeat steps 10–15 with a second cup.

THIS IS WHAT YOU SHOULD HAVE SO FAR.

BODY & NECK

16

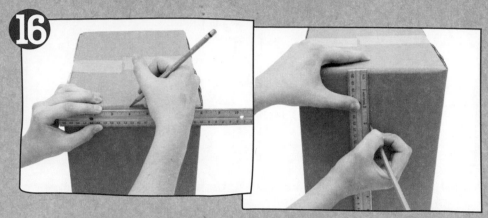

Seal both sides of the big box (the **BODY**) with packing tape and stand it on its short end. Determine where the **ARMS** will go. To do this, measure the width and divide it by 2 to find the midpoint. (Our box's side width is 8", so the midpoint would be 4".) Then measure 3" down from the midpoint. This will be your **ARM** hole.

17

Poke a starter hole through the mark with the tip of a sharp pencil, then widen the hole by wiggling the scissors up and down and side to side. Repeat steps 16–17 on the opposite side of the box.

18

To make the **NECK**, find the center of the **BODY**'s top end by making an "X" with your ruler from one corner to the other.

SHOULDERS,

19 Apply glue around the rim of a cup.

20 Attach the **NECK** to the center of the "X." Let glue dry completely.

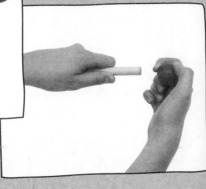

21 Unscrew the rod from a push-along toy. Be sure to remove the handle or knob if it has one.

22 Push the rod through the arm holes of the **BODY**. These are Boxbot's **SHOULDERS**.

23 For the **ARMS**, measure and mark a spot 1½" from one end of a paper towel tube.

ARMS & LEGS

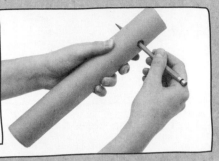

24 Poke a hole with a pushpin, then widen the hole with a pencil as shown. Push the pencil through the opposite side of the tube. You might want to use a pair of scissors to widen the hole even more (see step 17).

25 Attach **ARM** to the **SHOULDER** on both sides.

26 To make **LEGS**, gently peel open two mini boxes of cereal.

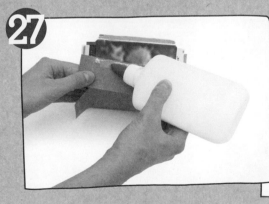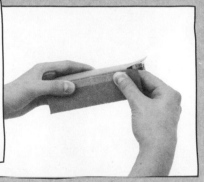

27 Glue the flaps and put the box back together inside out with the plain brown side exposed. Leave one end open.

28

Apply glue to the closed end.

29

Position **LEG** over center of **FOOT** and glue. Allow to dry.

30

Apply glue to the open flaps.

31

Attach the open flaps to the bottom of the **BODY**. Repeat steps 26–31 for the other **LEG** and **FOOT**. Let dry.

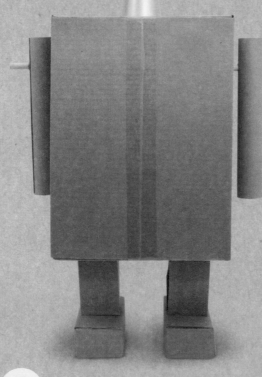

THIS IS WHAT YOU SHOULD HAVE SO FAR.

CONTROL PANEL

32 Cut a scrap of cardboard, about 3" x 5".

33 Measure and mark lines at $\frac{1}{2}$", $1\frac{1}{2}$", $3\frac{1}{2}$", $4\frac{1}{2}$".

34 Fold at each line to form a box. Apply mounting tape.

35 Attach to the inside of a small open box. This will be Boxbot's **CONTROL PANEL**.

36 Repeat steps 5–8 with the last cup and attach down to the **CONTROL PANEL**.

37 Remove the plastic jewels from rings. A pushpin might help you do this.

38 Apply mounting tape to the jewels. Cut away the excess tape.

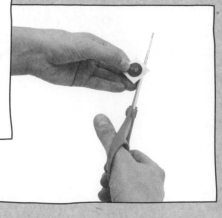

39 Attach the jewels to the **CONTROL PANEL.**

40

Apply mounting tape to the control panel. Attach **CONTROL PANEL** to the chest area of Boxbot.

41 Place **HEAD** onto the **BODY**, setting the neck hole over the **NECK.**

EXTRAS

Here's another version of Boxbot, using smaller boxes and different shapes. A takeout container makes a great head and I found some small scraps of cardboard that looked just like hands! If you find pieces of cardboard that you'd like to cut into certain shapes, make sure you ask a parent for help.

STYR

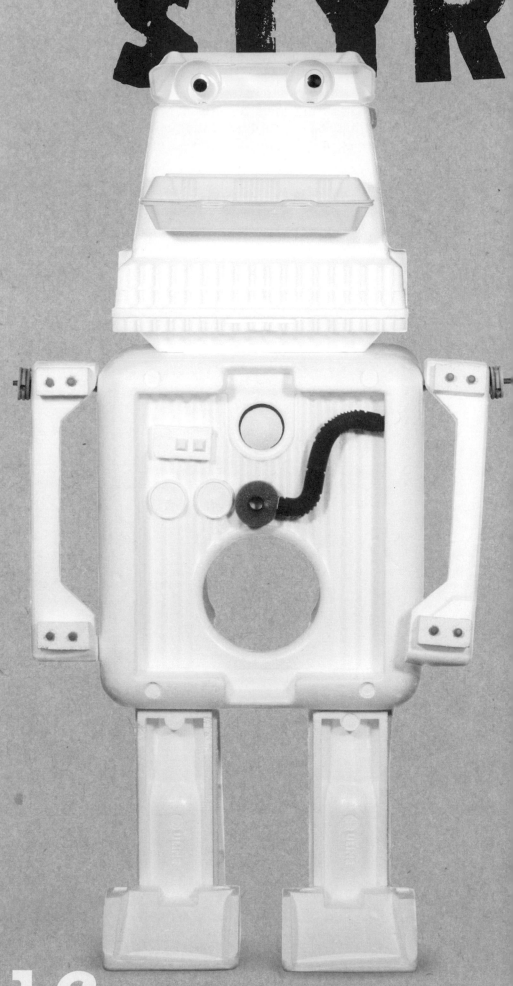

116 RECYCLED ROBOTS

OBOT

STYROBOT IS BIG. Really big. He might even be taller than you! This is advanced robotmaking: Styrobot's size and shape depend on the types of packing foam you uncover. Once you've gathered enough pieces, grab a sketch pad and draw out some design plans using this version as a guide. You can add cardboard boxes instead of packing foam, an old extension cord for the control panel wires, or pencils for joints.

RECYCLED MATERIALS
* Assorted pieces of packing foam:
  HEAD: 1 medium piece with a lid (I used a cooler from the grocery store.)
  FACE: 2 takeout sandwich containers
  4 miscellaneous small pieces
  ARMS: 2 long, thin pieces of equal size
  LEGS: 2 long, thick pieces of equal size (I used two thinner pieces bound together to make one piece.)
  FEET: 2 small pieces of equal size
  BODY: 1 big piece (I used one that came with a computer.)
* 2 foam rockets
* 2 plastic cups
* 8 NERF® darts
* 2 foam cups
* Miscellaneous packing foam pieces, for control panel
* Foam pool noodle
* Toy singing tube or whistling tube
* Assorted TINKERTOY parts, including 2 rods and 2 wheels

MATERIALS IN KIT
* Mounting tape (cut to size)
* 2 googly eyes

TOOLS NEEDED
* Pencil
* Ruler
* Scissors
* 2 brass fasteners
* White glue

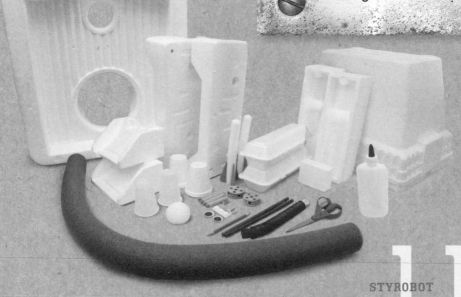

EYES & HEAD

1 Cut away the tips and the ends of a foam rocket, leaving a 4" length of tube.

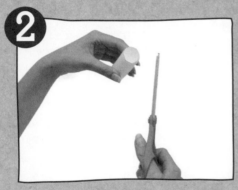

2 Apply mounting tape to both ends of the tube. Cut away the excess tape.

3 Apply a googly eye to one end of the foam rocket. This will be Styrobot's EYE.

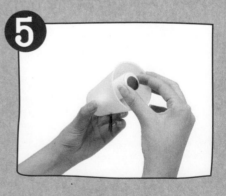

4 Make a hole in the middle of a plastic cup with a brass fastener. Insert the fastener through the hole from the inside so that the prongs are hanging down.

5 Attach the googly eye foam rocket into the bottom of the cup. Repeat steps 1–5 with the second cup.

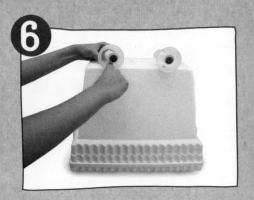

6

Attach the **EYES** to the bottom of the cooler (this is Styrobot's **HEAD**) by pressing the brass fasteners through the cooler's surface.

7

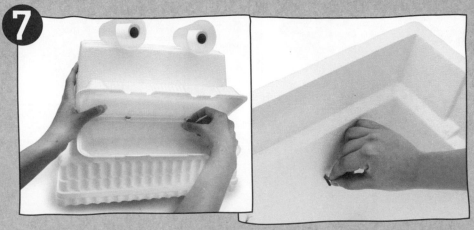

Press two more brass fasteners through the hinge of the takeout container (the **MOUTH**), and attach to the **HEAD**, bending the prongs inside as shown.

8

Apply mounting tape around the edge of the top of the cooler top. Attach the **HEAD** to the taped surface as shown.

9

THIS IS WHAT YOU SHOULD HAVE SO FAR.

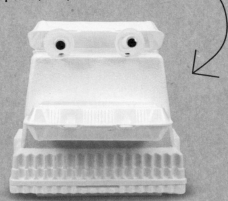

Apply mounting tape to the hinge of a second takeout container. This will be Styrobot's eyebrow.

ARMS & LEGS

10

Make two holes in a small piece of foam using a sharp pencil or scissors. These will be for the **ARM** bolts. You can place them wherever looks good.

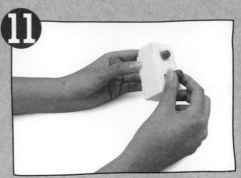

11

Insert NERF darts (or equivalent) into the holes. Repeat steps 10–11 three more times.

12

Apply mounting tape.

13

Attach the small pieces to each end of the **ARM** pieces.

THIS IS WHAT YOU SHOULD HAVE SO FAR.

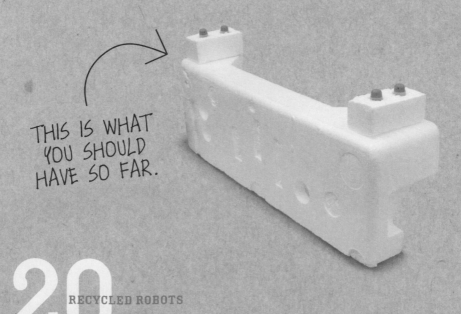

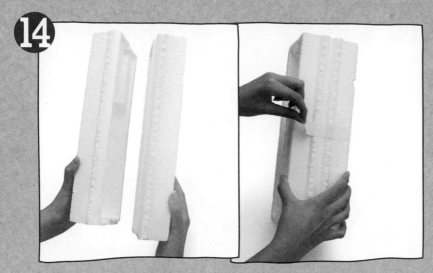

14

Assemble your **LEGS**. We taped two long pieces together to make a solid block. You may find leg pieces that are big enough on their own. Just make sure they are thick and sturdy enough to hold Styrobot's **BODY**.

15

Apply mounting tape to **FEET** and attach one to each **LEG** as shown.

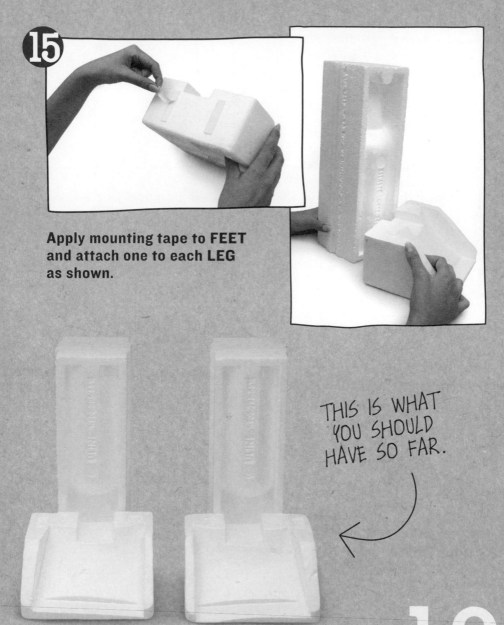

THIS IS WHAT YOU SHOULD HAVE SO FAR.

CONTROL PANEL

16 Measure and mark 1$^1/_2$" from the bottom of a cup. Repeat this four or five times around the diameter of the cup. These will be part of the **CONTROL PANEL**.

17 Connect your marks so they make an even circle around the cup. This will be the cut line.

18 Trim along the cut line.

19 Glue along the cut side of the cup.

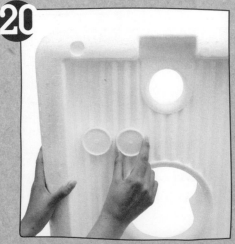

20 Attach cups to the large piece of foam (the **BODY**) wherever you think looks good. Hold for a minute until the cups dry.

21 Attach three small pieces of foam to a rectangle of foam.

22 Apply mounting tape to the back.

23 Attach the foam rectangle with three small pieces of foam above the cups.

24 Apply mounting tape to a foam ball.

25 Attach foam ball to the BODY.

26 Cut about 2" slice off of a foam pool noodle.

27 Apply mounting tape to the foam noodle slice.

28 Twist in a toy whistling tube into the side of the foam slice. You'll have to push hard.

29

Twist the other end into the BODY.

30

Attach the noodle slice to the BODY.

31

Line the ARM up with Styrobot's SHOULDER. With a sharp pencil, pierce through both the ARM and the BODY.

32

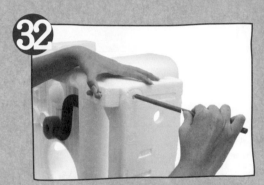

Widen the hole by wiggling the pencil and attach the ARM with a TINKERTOY rod (or equivalent).

33

Cap with a TINKERTOY wheel. Repeat steps 31–33 for the other ARM.

34

Apply mounting tape to the top of the LEGS.

35

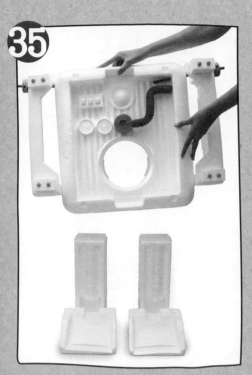

Attach the **BODY**
to the **LEGS**.

36

Apply mounting tape to top of
the **BODY**.

37

Attach the
HEAD to the
BODY.

MAKE IT GO!

Making Styrobot is one of the hardest projects in the book. So it would follow that making Styrobot move is also pretty hard. You'll need a Roomba vacuum cleaner, some extra pieces of foam, and a lot of patience. Don't get frustrated if your first idea doesn't work. Take a deep breath and try another way. That's what a robotic engineer would do!

A THE PLATFORM

You'll need to build a stable platform that can sit atop the Roomba and support the weight of Styrobot.

B THE SUPPORTS

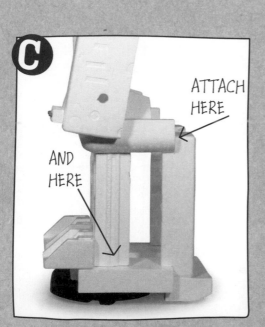

C ATTACH HERE

AND HERE

Once you have the platform in place, you need to build a support so Styrobot doesn't fall forward or backward. Make sure that the support attaches to both Styrobot and the platform.

EXTRAS

Here's a great example of how totally different pieces of foam can make a version of Styrobot with a personality and look all his own.

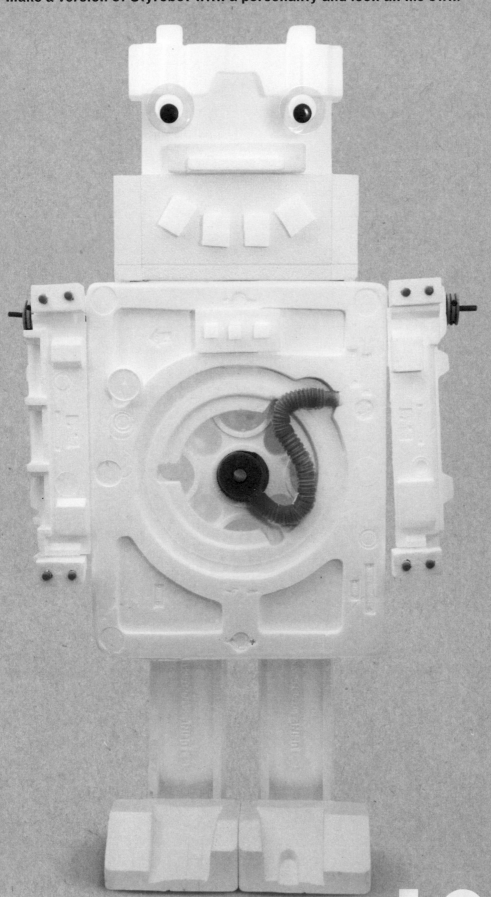

Jumpingjackbot's arms and legs are connected. They are powered by a motorized piston that makes them go up and down in a jumping-jack motion.

Eyes are connected to the center column, which is also connected to the arms.

CHAPTER 04

ROBOTS FROM ROBERT'S WORK-SHOP

"All of the robots in this chapter are made using recycled parts or my own templates. To me, they all have their own individual personalities."

TRANSBOT

"Transbot is made up of mostly transparent objects."

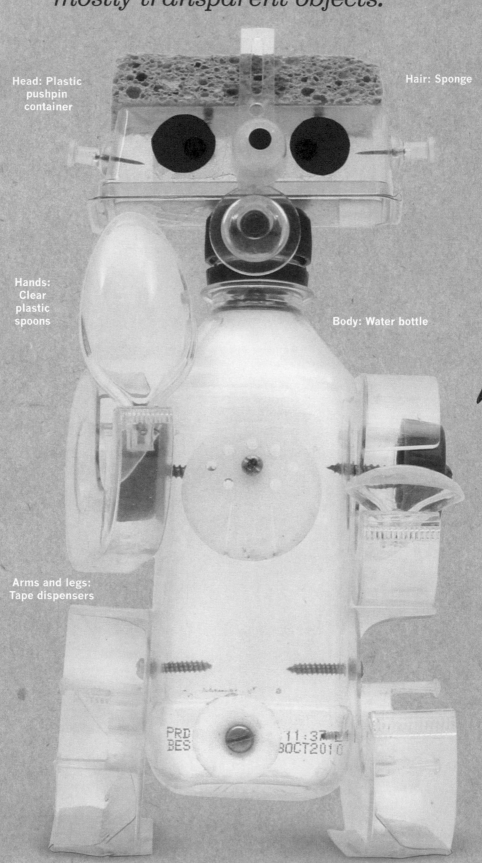

Head: Plastic pushpin container

Hair: Sponge

Hands: Clear plastic spoons

Body: Water bottle

Arms and legs: Tape dispensers

CANBOT

Head: Cut cardboard gift box

Face shields: Bottle caps

Arms: Cut cardboard box

Hands: Forks

"Canbot started his life as a coffee can."

Legs: Bent spoons

GREENBOT

Hair: Scrub brush

"I tried to use as many green objects as possible to make Greenie."

Head: Upside-down aspirin bottle

Body: Tomato soup can

Fingers: Cut straws

Feet: Jelly jar lids

3272

FORKBOT

"I find bent forks make very expressive robot hands"

Shoulders: Bottle caps

Body: Soup can

673N

Arms and hands: Forks

Belt: Inside parts of a telephone

Legs: Spoons

ADAMBOT

Headgear: Bottle cap

Face and assorted armor: Cardboard

"Adambot started off as a superhero action figure."

Chestplate:
Top of a tin can

EVEBOT

Body, arms, and legs:
Rolled cardboard

"Evebot was inspired by one of my favorite movie robots of all time, the one in Metropolis."

SPINBOT

"Spinbot uses a motor inside to make it spin around."

Head revolves,
powered by a motor
hidden in the base

STRAWBOT

"All of Strawbot's joints are connected with straws."

Strawbot was the inspiration for Cupbot's arms.

I hope the robots in this book inspire you to make your own great recycled robots Visit MakeRecycledRobots.com and send me a picture or video.

Yours in imagining,

Bob Malone